Searchlights for Spelling Year 4 Pupil's Book

Chris Buckton   **Pie Corbett**

CAMBRIDGE
UNIVERSITY PRESS

A Is it n or nn? Write out the words, filling in the missing letters.

I love my gra__y.

The dog pi__ed for its owner.

When I get hungry I want to eat my di__er.

The po__y jumps really well.

The robbers were ru__ing away.

I need more mo__ey to buy the computer game.

I cannot play te__is very well.

The first past the line is the wi__er.

Write two more sentences of your own using one n word and one nn word.

B Is it m or mm, p or pp, s or ss? Write out the words, filling in the missing letters.

The bear had a pain in its tu__y so it went ho__e.

An a__le a day keeps the flu away.

I can see well with my gla__es so I'll put flowers in va__es.

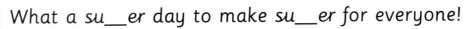

What a su__er day to make su__er for everyone!

We'll gather po__ies of red ro__es.

The crystal light shi__ers and makes sha__es on the floor.

We must send a me__age to say we'll be late.

Please pass me the salt and pe__er.

Write three more sentences of your own using m or mm, p or pp and s or ss words where you can.

C Make three lists of as many double consonant words as you can.

Adjectives	Nouns	Verbs
silly	rabbit	nibbled
	carrot	

Now write two puzzle sentences like the one below.
Give them to a friend to complete.

The s____y r_____t n_____d the c_____t.

Extra challenge
Some letters, such as h, are never doubled. How many others can you think of? Make a list.

A Which is the correct spelling? Write the correct words in a list.

Mr Kazoo did (knot/not) (no/know)
(wear/where) he was. It was months
since he had set (sale/sail) in his (knew/new)
boat, but now he was lost and did not
know when he (would/wood) get home.
He was (week/weak) and had not eaten (meet/meat) for
ages. He sniffed with his (nose/knows), searching for the
(scent/sent) of food. Then he gave a sudden (grown/groan).
(Eye/I) hate this (plaice/place), he thought.

Now choose two of the homophone pairs. Use both words in each
pair in a sentence.

B Write the correct words in a list.

I am going <u>two</u> town this <u>mourning</u>. <u>Wood</u> <u>ewe</u> like to come
<u>to</u>? If you do, that would make <u>too</u> of us. We will go <u>threw</u> the
shopping centre, <u>wear</u> <u>their</u> are lots of shops that <u>eye</u> like. At
the moment there is a <u>sail</u> <u>inn</u> my favourite shop. <u>There</u> clothes
are very <u>cheep</u> and you might <u>sea</u> something you like. If you
do, I will <u>by</u> it <u>four</u> you.

Can you continue this passage using more homophones? Write all
the possible spellings like this – to/too/two. Underline the correct
one.

C Some of the words in these adverts and headlines have the wrong spelling. Write the correct spellings in a list.

Dog's lost tale mystery

For aching mussels
Easi-rub
takes away the pane

SUPER SPECS SAIL
two pears for the price of one!

Sunny Skin Cream
cleans your paws

Take care – son getting hotter!

Soul sighted swimming in Thames

Now make up some of your own to swap with a friend.

Think about . . .

If you are unsure about spelling a homophone, then underline it and check later. Make a note of it in your spelling journal so you can check it next time you write it.

A Word subtraction.
Remove the ending ing and spell the root correctly.

swimming − ing = *swim*

going − ing =

shutting − ing =

picking − ing =

hoping − ing =

showing − ing =

getting − ing =

phoning − ing =

slipping − ing =

sliding − ing =

Make up two word subtractions of your own.

B Word addition.
Add on the ending ing. Think about how this might alter the spelling.

run + ing = *running*   race + ing =

rush + ing =   clean + ing =

come + ing =	tap + ing =
sit + ing =	place + ing =
move + ing =	bet + ing =
pop + ing =	spy + ing =

Now write each verb with an ed ending where possible.
Watch out for the catch-you-outs!

C Complete this poem about the Pied Piper of Hamelin. It describes all the rats following the Piper out of town. See how long you can make the poem, using different verbs.

The rats followed the Piper,

Tumbling, stumbling . . .

Find a way to include some s and ed verb endings.

rush   dive
           dart   dodge   race   run

Extra challenge

When you add ing onto a word ending in e, then you drop the e. When you add ing onto a word with a 'short' vowel before a final consonant, you double the consonant. Is this the same if you are adding ed? Make a list of words to see if it is.

A Match the present tense to the past tense.
Write out each pair like this – *tell/told*.

say   told   swim   came   wake

heard   said   fall   may   begun

leave   woke   come   dig   hear

tell   fell   dug   think   begin

Four words do not have a pair. Find them and write the past tense for each.

Check in a dictionary if you are not sure of the spelling.

B Change the underlined verbs into the past tense.
Make a list of the verbs like this – *creeps/crept*.

When Dr Foster was younger . . .

Dr Foster in his youth,
<u>Has</u> trouble even then.
He <u>writes</u> a lot of nonsense
And then he <u>hides</u> his pen.

He <u>creeps</u> along the carpet,
His feet <u>are</u> in a muddle.
He <u>weeps</u> into his hanky
Until he <u>makes</u> a puddle.

He <u>sings</u> a song at midnight
And <u>tells</u> a silly tale,
Then <u>eats</u> a loaf of bread
And <u>sleeps</u> upon a bale.

Use four of the past tense verbs in a sentence of your own.

Change the verbs into the past tense.
Make a list, writing each verb like
this – *make/made*.

Last night a gang of robbers make
their way to the field next to the bank.
They dig a deep pit. One falls in and
finds a tunnel. It is dark in the tunnel. Soon they are
all down there. Some bring spades. To keep themselves happy
they sing cheerful songs. They think they are safe. However,
a policewoman drives up in her car. She leaves the car and
strides across to the pit. She thinks that she can hear singing!

Are there any in the list that change in a similar way?

Extra challenge

See if you can find some past tense catch-you-outs for a
friend. Check them using a dictionary.

A Some nouns can be changed into adjectives by adding al.

I do not believe in <u>magic</u>.
My <u>magical</u> brother can fly.

Noun	Adjective
magic	magical

Write the noun and then the adjective in a list like this.

I enjoyed the (tropics) sun.

My (music) brother plays the violin.

Use your (mathematics) skills to solve the problem.

An (occasion) cream bun is nice to eat.

When my brother arrived I had to cook an (addition) egg.

Red Riding Hood is a (tradition) tale.

Now write a sentence of your own using an al adjective.

B Choose from these nouns and add the suffix al or ic to make the missing adjectives.

exception   nation   history   music   tradition
occasion   voice   sensation

Last January I went to an _____ show with my mates.
The concert was at The Old Vic Theatre which is a _____,

_____ building. It wasn't a _____ or anything _____ like that. It was a rock concert with unbelievable sounds and _____ rhythmic _____. It was _____.

C Solve these riddles. The word endings have been given in brackets to help you.

A room that holds many books. (ary)

The main city of a country is known as the ... (al)

If you are very ill, this is where you should be. (al)

Find this useful object at the side of a railway line. (al)

The shortest month. (ary)

Describes something made of metal. (ic)

Now invent more riddles, using words with the suffixes al, ary or ic. Give them to a friend to solve.

Extra challenge

Find the root words behind these words with suffixes

January   vocal   organic

A Make verbs from these nouns and adjectives. You will need to add
ate, en, ify or ise.

> *deep tough memory active note motive*

Choose three of the verbs and write a sentence for each.

B Add the correct suffix so that the sentence
makes sense. Use ate, en, ify, ise.

The Princess said that I had to (*apology*).

The King wanted to (*glory*) his son's ability to play hopscotch.

12

The unicorn had to (light) its load.

The mud had begun to (solid).

The sound of the giant had started to (deaf) the children.

The wizard told me that if the water was stale I would have to (pure) it.

Bees (pollen) flowers for us.

Write a sentence to explain what happens to words that end in e or y.

C Change these nouns and adjectives into verbs.

> quantity   category   special   straight   pollen
> sad   alien   fertile   length   drama

Check them in your dictionary. Write down the new words with their meanings like this.

Noun or adjective	Verb	Definition
loose	loosen	to make loose

Extra challenge

If the verb from <u>solid</u> is <u>solidify</u>, what is the verb from <u>liquid</u>?

A Read this poem. Each of the words in brackets needs the suffix ment or ness to make a noun. Write out the new word each time and note how the spelling has changed.

My dragon . . .

Can be full of (naughty),
Is known for her (bossy),
Is not known for (tidy)!
But she gives me (encourage),
Is graceful in (move) and full of (kind).

Now write more about the dragon. Use ment and ness words.

B Add the suffix ness or ment to the words in brackets to make a noun. Write them in a chart like the one on page 15.
Underline words that you have to change when you add the suffix.
Add some more examples of ness and ment words to the chart.

Tim's (slow) was a result of the (enchant).
Bill's (careful) made the new (develop) a success.
The (foolish) of the (govern) brought disaster.
The new (replace) was sacked for (clumsy).

Too much (excite) leads to (dizzy).

Word	Add *ment* or *ness*
quick	quickness
greedy	greediness

C Each line of this poem has a word ending in ish. It also plays with the idea of opposites and impossibilities (for example, a flattish hill!)

Wishing poem

I wish I was . . .   a giant that was smallish,
a hill that was flattish,   a sun that was bluish.

Add ish to the words below and use them to make up a Wishing poem of your own.

baby   red   child   round
slug   large   style   fool

Complete this chart, adding the words you used in your poem.
Can you see any spelling patterns?

Adjective	Adding *ish*
flat	double the *t*
small	just add *ish*
blue	

Extra challenge

Look at these words. Can you work out what the suffix craft means?

woodcraft   needlecraft   handicraft   stagecraft

A Complete the addition sums. The first is done for you.

loaf + loaf   =   loaves   cuff + cuff   =

half + half   =   roof + roof   =

shelf + shelf =   knife + knife   =

scarf + scarf =   wife + wife   =

wolf + wolf   =   chief + chief   =

Write three more sums like these.
Choose a word and write it in the singular and in the plural
in the same sentence, like this one.

The shelf looked strong, but the set of shelves
looked stronger.

B Change the spelling of the underlined
words so that there is more than one.

Jack strolled to the market.
In his pocket he had plenty of golden coins.
He bought one brown calf,
And one woolly scarf,
One sharp knife,
From one lean wife,
One big chief,
And a new belief.

Decide what else would need changing to read the poem with the plurals.

Finish this second verse using plural nouns: *On the way home he . . .*

Rewrite the passage, changing each plural to the singular.
What else needs changing so that it makes sense in the singular?

Dear Doctor Stoby,

Last night the village was attacked by <u>elves</u>. We saw white <u>puffs</u> of smoke drifting over the <u>roofs</u>. So, we took our weapons from the <u>shelves</u> and made <u>ourselves</u> ready. There were a few <u>sniffs</u>, but most of us were prepared. Then the <u>elves</u> fired rockets. They made many <u>swerves</u> through the air. We ran for our <u>lives</u> to the caves in the <u>cliffs</u>. The <u>elves</u> will never make us their slaves! Please send <u>loaves</u> of bread and more bandages.

In haste, Pedro

Extra challenge

These catch-you-outs can be spelled either way.

<u>dwarfs</u> or <u>dwarves</u>   <u>hoofs</u> or <u>hooves</u>

Can you find any other examples?

A Is it *ight* or *ite*? Make a list of the missing words.

She flew the _____ high in the sky.

The ghost gave them a _____ .

Get him to hospital – it's a snake _____ !

What do you think? It looks about _____ .

Can you come out tonight? I _____ .

Good _____ everyone. Sleep _____ .

They had a _____ when they found the old bomb

_____ .

I love being in the spot _____ and it's so _____ !

Here is one mnemonic for remembering the *ight* ending.

Iguanas **G**o **H**oppi-**T**y

Write your own mnemonic for *ight*.

B *They turned on the light and it gave them a fright. They saw . . .*

Finish the sentence and continue the writing with as many ight or ite words as possible.

C Brainstorm ight and ough words. Make two lists.
Think of another common word ending and make a third list.

Write a mnemonic for each of your common endings. Use words from the three lists to write some sentences.

ough	ight	
tough	might	

Extra challenge

Write down the root words for each underlined word.

The boy stared at the <u>invention</u>. It was made to <u>perfection</u> and caught his <u>attention</u>. The <u>construction</u> was amazing. Its <u>attraction</u> was magnetic. He wanted no <u>interruption</u>.

A Match the prefix to the root word. Watch out for the catch-you-outs.

Write a sentence using two of the words.

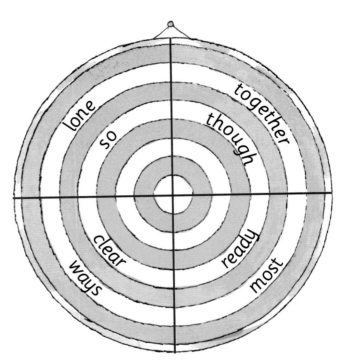

lone
so
though
together
clear
ways
ready
most

B Write the missing al words in this passage.

_____ we tried we could not make them hear us as we had _____ gone too far. At one point we _____ managed, but they turned in the opposite direction. We _____ stayed close together but this time we had forgotten. We were all _____. Whatever could we do? Then we heard an _____ CRASH!

Finish the passage with a few sentences. Try to use al words.

C Complete the spelling of these al prefix words.

A word that describes a god or something huge.

To do something with a group of people.

To nearly do something.

To add something.

All the time.

To have done something before.

Make up some more al or ad word riddles of your own.
○ Test them on a friend.

Think about . . .

If you are unsure about how to spell a word, think about whether it has any prefixes or suffixes. Try these:
- Listen to the syllables of the word.
- Think of another word that has a similar beginning or ending.
- Think about its meaning.

A Read these words aloud. Add the prefix un to each of them. Say the new word. Work out what it means. Then write the new word and its meaning in your spelling log. Title the page <u>Prefixes</u>.

known   tidy   able   important

usual   natural   wanted

B Add the prefix over to these words. Write the new words and their meanings in your spelling log.

run   lap   kill   heat   haul   flow

Find some more to add to your list.

C Use these prefixes to make new words. Check them in your dictionary. Write the words and their meanings in your spelling log.

pre
post
sub
inter

Do the same root words go with pre and post?

Extra challenge

There are over 30 common prefixes in English. You can spot them in your dictionary by looking for the hyphen. How many can you find? Make a list.

A Read the words with wa and wo letter strings.
Practise **Look Say Cover Write Check**.

wa		wo	
Beginning	Middle	Beginning	Middle
walk	swap	word	swore

Write out the chart and find another word for each column.
You could use your reading book to search for words.

B Work with a partner. Brainstorm some words for each letter
string in the chart.

wi	wo	wa
wicked	worried	award
wizard		

Use these words to make up a short story about a <u>wicked wizard</u>.

C Work with a partner. Brainstorm some words which contain the
letter string wi.

Is swi a common pattern?

What other letters can go in front of wi?

Can they go in front of wa and wo as well?

○ Can you find any words with the letter string wu?

Extra challenge

Can wo or wa ever come at the end of a word?

A Copy this chart. Say the words out loud.

back	trick	park	talk	blink	silk

Think of some rhyming words and write them under the headings.
Underline the last two letters of each word. What do you notice?

B Where is k in these words?
Copy the chart and sort the words.

think   kerb   kitten   woke

clock   walk   tackle   make   kettle

Add more rhyming
words of your own
for the <u>End</u> column.
Write down three things
you have found out.

Beginning	Middle	End

C Read the poem and look out for words with k.

In my pack of tricks I have . . .
a broken kettle,
a speckled cracker,
a wrinkled pickle,
a kindly kitten,
and a milk drink.

Copy the chart and sort the words. Do you notice any patterns? Make up some more lines with k objects for your pack of tricks.

Beginning	Middle	End

Extra challenge

Can you find any words that end with a vowel + k?
Some clues:
a type of canoe   a hairy animal   you can cook a stir-fry in one

A Which is the odd one out in this list?

window   show   flow   town

blow   below

Make two lists in
your spelling log.
Write some more
words for each list.

ow *as in how*	ow *as in low*

B Ou can make at least four different sounds. Two of them are in the last sentence!

Copy the chart into your spelling log. Find more words for each heading. Some have been filled in to help you get started.

'short' oo	or	ow	er
would	your	out	journey

Which is the most common phoneme to represent ou?
Which is the least common?

C The ough letter string can make a lot of different sounds.
Read these words and sort them into rhyming pairs.
Which is the odd one out?

cough   plough   through

trough   bought   fought

enough   rough   bough

Write the words into lists
according to their sound.
Find more ough words and
add them to your lists.
Can you make any other
rhyming pairs?

I've
gone through
enough!

Extra challenge

Find as many words as you can that end in eight.
How are they pronounced? Make up a sentence to help
you remember them.

A Read these sentences. Each uses two words with the same root. Write the words down and underline the root each time.
Can you think of more words with the same root? Add them to your list.

I was impressed by the speed
of the express train.

The book is very readable but you might misread
the last sentence.

I recounted my adventures but missed out the bit about
counting the pirates' gold coins.

The octet played the music an octave higher than usual.

B Write a sentence for each of these words. Underline the common root in each word. Can you work out what the root means? Use a dictionary to help you.

tractor   contract   extract

Now do the same for this set of words.

mortal   mortify   mortgage

C Read the sets of words. Write them down and underline the common root in each set. Write sentences for each set of words.

spectator   spectacles   spectacular

manuscript   prescription   describe

finale   finalise   finite

Extra challenge

Invent some new words by adding a prefix or suffix to common roots, for example:

malphone — to send a rude phone message

Some prefixes and suffixes you could use:

sub   dis   mal   tele   able   ship   ness   ment

A Make an adverb from each of these adjectives. Write the sums and the new words.

Don't forget the rule:

If the word ends in consonant + y, change the y to an i.

helpful   + ly =
quick   + ly =
silly   + ly =
sleepy   + ly =
funny   + ly =

Now think of some sums of your own. Add them to the list.

B Change these verbs to adjectives by adding the suffix ful or ive. Write the new words down. Don't forget to drop the e if the suffix starts with a vowel; keep the e if it starts with a consonant.

thank   wonder   attract   play
hope   respect   act   decorate

Turn the adjectives into adverbs by adding ly.

C Change these verbs to nouns by adding ure or ment.
Don't forget the rule:

> Drop the e if the suffix starts with a vowel; keep the e if it starts with a consonant.

press
encourage
please
expose
measure
replace
pay
advertise
depart
sculpt

What do you notice about the endings of words that take the suffix ure?

Choose five of the new words and write a sentence for each.

Extra challenge

The suffix able can make an adjective from a verb. Can you think of any examples? Here are two to help you get started.

adorable   breakable

A ible and able are useful suffixes. But it's hard to remember which is which!
Read the words. Sort them into two sets.
Work with a partner to do **Look Say Cover Write Check**.

Together, work out the root of each word. Are there any odd ones? How does the root change when the suffix is added? Make a note of the changes in your spelling log.

horrible	breakable	agreeable
terrible	probable	possible
suitable	reliable	miserable
	forgivable	

B Can you add able or ible to these roots to make a new word?
Take care with the spelling! Use a dictionary to check.
Write them in your spelling log. Use each of the words in a sentence.

value	force
sense	envy
reverse	respect
afford	identify
honour	enjoy

C Can you add *ion* to these verbs to make a new noun? Take care with the spelling! Is it *tion* or *sion*? Use a dictionary to check. Write the new words in your spelling log with their meanings.

provide	navigate	supervise
prevent	punctuate	divide
collect	vibrate	confuse
conclude	vary	collide

Think about . . .

Sometimes the best way of remembering whether it's *able* or *ible* is by checking whether the word <u>looks</u> right. Write out both spellings and go for the one that looks familiar!

A Write down these words and put a ring round the prefix or suffix which means <u>small</u>.
Write down the meaning of each word. Use a dictionary to help you.
Find some more 'small' words with these prefixes or suffixes.

kitchenette
leaflet
gosling
duckling
miniskirt
minibus

B Join up each root with a prefix or suffix to make a new word. Use the words in sentences.

mini   duck   chip   ette

micro   major   scope   ling

beast   disk

Now make up some new <u>small</u> words of your own, for example:

lunchette – a small meal

C Think of as many words as you can which start with mini or micro. Use a dictionary to help you. Make a list. Find out which languages mini and micro come from.

Make up some new <u>small</u> words of your own using mini and micro, for example:

minisleep — a nap

Extra challenge

Can you find out the meaning of <u>nanosecond</u>?

A Rule four columns on a page of your spelling log.

B Rule five columns on a page of your spelling log.
C Copy Blake's headings.

Look through your work for some words you find hard to spell.

A Find four spelling errors.

Word	Reason for error/ tricky bit	What to do	Correct spelling

B Find five spelling errors. Identify the tricky bit each time and find another word with the same spelling pattern.

Word	Reason for error/ tricky bit	What to do	Correct spelling	Word with the same spelling pattern

C Find six spelling errors. Identify the tricky bit each time and find other words with the same spelling pattern.

Word	Reason for error/ tricky bit	What to do	Correct spelling	Word with the same spelling pattern

If I don't know a spelling I write it out in different ways and go for the one that looks right.

Think about . . .

Is there one kind of error you make more often than other kinds? Is it an eye, ear, hand or brain error?

A Match up each word with a suffix to make an adjective.
Check the words in your dictionary.

> wash
> baby
> friend
> power
> drama

> ish   ly   ic   ful   able

Make a list of the new words.
Use each word in a sentence.

B Change these nouns into adjectives. Check them in your
dictionary. Use each new word in a sentence.

> horror
> base
> energy
> greed
> hatred

> ic   ing   y   ful

Can you find a verb with the same root for each word?

C Sort these words into nouns and verbs. Then change each one to make an adjective. Write them out in a chart like this. Watch out for the catch-you-outs. Sometimes the noun and verb are the same, and sometimes there's no verb.

Verb	Noun	Adjective
enjoy	enjoyment	enjoyable

differ   shock   argument   suspicion

loneliness   electricity   imagine   digit

○ Find some more words of your own to add to the columns.

Extra challenge

Can you make three adjectives from the noun <u>terror</u>?

A Write out the dialogue between Ben and Petra, shortening the underlined words to contractions. Then add some more dialogue of your own.

> "<u>I am</u> not coming to the disco," explained Ben, "because I <u>do not</u> like dancing. <u>We will</u> go skateboarding instead."

> "I <u>cannot</u> go. I <u>must not</u> go into town without asking my mum."

B

"Tom, I've had enough! I'm always telling you to tidy your room and you've done nothing about it!" shouted Mr Harding.

Read the speech bubble. Write out the contractions like this: I've = I have. Write Tom's reply to his father. Use as many contractions as you can.

C Read the passage carefully. Some apostrophes are contractions, and some show who something belongs to (possession). Write them out in two lists. Write down the meaning of each one. Then continue the Inspector's speech, using as many apostrophes as you can.

> "I can't find the missing murder weapon," sighed Inspector Fonz. "Mrs Brown's scarf was found in Professor White's desk but he's got an alibi. He'll be able to clear his name. I shouldn't think he'll be a likely suspect."

contraction	possession
can't	

Extra challenge

Make a reminder card so that you won't forget which <u>its</u> (<u>its</u> or <u>it's</u>?) it is! Use the card as a bookmark in your spelling log.

Useful words

Which words do you find tricky? Write them in your spelling log.
Add more tricky words to your list when you find them.
Practise **Look Say Cover Write Check**.

Key words

above	can't	I'm	place	tries
across	change	inside	right	turn(ed)
almost	coming	jumped	round	under
along	didn't	knew	second	until
also	different	know	show	upon
always	does	leave	sometimes	used
any	don't	might	started	walk(ed)(ing)
around	during	morning	still	watch
ask(ed)	every	much	stopped	where
before	first	near	such	while
below	following	never	suddenly	without
better	found	number	think	woke(n)
between	goes	often	thought	write
began	gone	only	through	year
being	half	opened	today	young
both	heard	other	together	
brought	high	outside	told	

ODDBODS

across	different	might	their	thought
any	don't	other	there	told
asked	electricity	stopped	they're	under
being	guess	suddenly	think	until
change	half	sure	though	

Months of the year

January	July
February	August
March	September
April	October
May	November
June	December

Words for English

adjective	homonym
apostrophe	homophone
connective	hyphen
diminutive	pun
font	simile

Words for science

battery	liquid
condition	organism
consumer	resistance
dissolve	solidify
friction	solution
habitat	temperature
key	vertebrate

Words for instruction

classify	justify
construct	plot
convert	state

Numbers

thousand	tenth
ten thousand	twelfth
million	twentieth
fifth	hundredth
sixth	thousandth
eighth	

Words for maths

apex	millennium
area	millimetre
bar chart	prime number
circumference	reflection
co-ordinates	roman numeral
database	rotation
divisible by	spiral
imperial unit	square number
inverse	sub-set
magic square	translation
metric unit	vertex
mile	

Having problems spelling a word?

Try these ideas . . .

- What sounds can you hear? Which letters could spell each sound?
- Break the word into syllables. Remember, every syllable has a vowel or a y in it.
- Try different ways of spelling the word. Which one looks right?
- Think of words with the same sort of pattern, e.g. <u>true</u>, <u>blue</u>.
- Think of words with the same meanings, e.g. <u>ear</u>, <u>hear</u>, <u>heard</u>.
- Are there any prefixes or suffixes?
- Is there a rule that you know, e.g. when you add ing?
- Is there a mnemonic? e.g. there is a <u>hen</u> in <u>when</u>.
- Use a dictionary or spellchecker or work with a spelling partner.
- Underline the word and check it later.
- Never dodge a useful word – have your best go and keep writing!

Your spelling log

Start a spelling log to help you remember words you need to learn. You can put these things in your spelling log:

- words you often get wrong;
- ways to remember tricky words; useful spelling tips;
- things you have learned about spelling;
- words to learn for the week;
- investigations; word collections;
- prefixes, suffixes.

Learning new words

Practise **Look Say Cover Write Check**.

Look

- Look at the shape of the word.
- Make a picture of the word in your mind.
- Look at the letter patterns that make up each sound.
- Break the word into syllables.
- Look for words within the word.

Say

- Say the whole word.
- Say the beginning sound.
- Say the end sound.
- Say the middle part of the word.
- Say the letter names.
- Say the whole word again.
- Over-pronounce any parts that you might forget.

Cover

- Cover the word.
- Picture the word in your mind.
- Hold it in your mind as if it's on a TV screen.

Write

- Write the word in joined writing.
- Think about the picture in your mind as you write.
- Say the letter names or the sounds.

Check

- If it isn't right yet, try again!
- Think about why you got it wrong.
- Look at the tricky bits.
- Underline the tricky bits.

A few helpful hints

Double consonants

If the first syllable in a word is 'long', then use one consonant (<u>biter</u>). If it is 'short', use two consonants (<u>bitter</u>).

Changing words ending in f to the plural

- Most words ending in f simply add s (<u>roof</u> – <u>roofs</u>).
- Some words ending in f change to ves (<u>thief</u> – <u>thieves</u>).
- Words ending in ff just add s (<u>cliffs</u>).
- Words ending in fe change to ves (<u>wife</u> – <u>wives</u>).

Suffixes

- When you add consonant suffixes ly, ful
  – most words stay the same (<u>bad</u> – <u>badly</u>, <u>fear</u> – <u>fearful</u>)
  – words ending in y change the y to i (<u>beauty</u> – <u>beautiful</u>)
- When you add a vowel suffix like ic, ist or ive to a word ending in e or y, drop the e or y from the base word (<u>base</u> – <u>basic</u>).
- ible or able? If the word contains a recognisable verb, the ending is often able. There are exceptions to this (<u>reversible</u> is one of them!).
- When adding ion:
  – tion is more common than sion and is often preceded by an a (<u>identification</u>) or any consonant other than s (<u>attention</u>).
  – sion is used in words ending in d/de or s/se (<u>conclude</u> – <u>conclusion</u>).